WHERE ARE THEY?

CRYPTS MADE WHILE-U-WAIT.

GROSS STUFF

DID YOU DO YOUR HOMEWORK?

I'LL BE HOME FOR BREAKFAST

FIND FREDDIE & LISA IN THE HAUNTED HOUSE

MONSTER MADNESS

MORE THAN
1,000
FUN THINGS TO
SEARCH AND
FIND

FOUR BOOKS IN ONE
By
Anthony Tallarico

CREEPY CASTLE

INSTANT MUD!

kidsbooks
Incorporated

FIND FRANKIE & HIS MONSTER FRIENDS

Visit us at www.kidsbooks.com

FIND FREDDIE & LISA

IN THE

HAUNTED HOUSE

Freddie and Lisa have discovered a house that's unlike any other...a haunted house!

FIND FREDDIE & LISA AT THE HAUNTED HOUSE AND...

☐ Apples (2)
☐ Apron
☐ Baseball cap
☐ Bats (2)
☐ Bones (3)
☐ Box
☐ Burned-out candle
☐ Clothespin
☐ Coffeepot
☐ Crown
☐ Dog
☐ Dracula
☐ Duck
☐ Eyeglasses
☐ Faucet
☐ Fish tank
☐ Fishing pole
☐ Ghosts (3)
☐ Hammer
☐ Heart
☐ Kite
☐ Light bulb
☐ Lips
☐ Mouse
☐ Mummy
☐ Owl
☐ Paint bucket
☐ Paper bag
☐ Peanut
☐ Pencils (2)
☐ Piggy bank
☐ Question mark
☐ Saw
☐ Scarves (2)
☐ Sock
☐ Straw
☐ Submarine
☐ Tire
☐ Truck
☐ Umbrella

Should they go in?
Should they not go in?
What do you think
they should do?

FIND FREDDIE &
LISA BEFORE
THEY DECIDE
AND...

- ☐ Birds (2)
- ☐ Black paint
- ☐ Blimps (2)
- ☐ Bowling ball
- ☐ Box
- ☐ Broom
- ☐ Burned-out bulb
- ☐ Cactus
- ☐ Camel
- ☐ Candle
- ☐ Chef's hat
- ☐ Feather
- ☐ Flower
- ☐ Football
- ☐ Giant straw
- ☐ Giraffe
- ☐ Jester
- ☐ King
- ☐ Laundry
- ☐ License plate
- ☐ Longest hair
- ☐ Lost boot
- ☐ Lost mask
- ☐ Mustache
- ☐ Napoleon
- ☐ Painted egg
- ☐ Rabbit
- ☐ Rain cloud
- ☐ Red wagon
- ☐ Sailboat
- ☐ Short pants
- ☐ Skull
- ☐ Sled
- ☐ Slide
- ☐ Star
- ☐ Top hats (2)
- ☐ Trash can
- ☐ Umbrella
- ☐ Who can't go?

Ready...Set...Go!!
Everyone runs toward
the door of the haunted
house...but only
two enter!

FIND FREDDIE &
LISA AS THEY
MEET THE
MONSTERS AND...

☐ Apple
☐ Arrow
☐ Bag
☐ Balloon
☐ Banana peel
☐ Baseball cap
☐ Bodiless head
☐ Bone
☐ Boot
☐ Bows (3)
☐ Broken heart
☐ Broom
☐ Cake
☐ Can
☐ Candles (5)
☐ Clothesline
☐ Crystal ball
☐ Earrings
☐ Eyeglasses
☐ Fish
☐ Flower
☐ Four-eyed monster
☐ Genie
☐ Ghosts (2)
☐ Ice-cream cone
☐ Lightning
☐ Necktie
☐ Number 13
☐ Owl
☐ Piano
☐ Roller skates
☐ Santa Claus
☐ Six-fingered hand
☐ Skulls (5)
☐ Snake
☐ Spoon
☐ Tombstone
☐ Watering can
☐ Worms (2)

Ms. Witch makes monstrous snacks. Her specialty is the "Everything Goes" sandwich!

FIND FREDDIE & LISA AT SNACK TIME AND...

- ☐ Accordion
- ☐ Apple
- ☐ Baseball
- ☐ Bell
- ☐ Blackbird
- ☐ Bone
- ☐ Brush
- ☐ Candle
- ☐ Checkerboard
- ☐ Drill
- ☐ Earring
- ☐ Faucet
- ☐ Fish (2)
- ☐ Flower
- ☐ Fork
- ☐ Frying pan
- ☐ Grapes
- ☐ Green cup
- ☐ Heart
- ☐ Helmet
- ☐ Ice-cream cone
- ☐ Ladle
- ☐ Mustaches (2)
- ☐ Neckties (2)
- ☐ Oil can
- ☐ Orange
- ☐ Palm tree
- ☐ Pear
- ☐ Polka-dotted handkerchief
- ☐ Rolling pin
- ☐ Saw
- ☐ Scissors
- ☐ Sock
- ☐ Stool
- ☐ Straw
- ☐ Toaster
- ☐ TV set
- ☐ Watermelon
- ☐ Wooden spoon

Freddie & Lisa begin to explore the haunted house. A wrong turn and...down, down, down they tumble.

FIND FREDDIE & LISA IN THE DUNGEON AND...

- ☐ Airplane
- ☐ Balloon
- ☐ Banana peel
- ☐ Bomb
- ☐ Book
- ☐ Bowling ball
- ☐ Broken egg
- ☐ Broom
- ☐ Candy cane
- ☐ Corn
- ☐ Cupcake
- ☐ Doctor
- ☐ Drum
- ☐ Fire hydrant
- ☐ Flowerpot
- ☐ Flying bat
- ☐ Football
- ☐ Hammer
- ☐ Hot dog
- ☐ Ice-cream cone
- ☐ Ice-cream pop
- ☐ Mummies (3)
- ☐ Piggy bank
- ☐ Rabbit
- ☐ Racer
- ☐ Roller skates
- ☐ Scarecrow
- ☐ School bag
- ☐ Shark
- ☐ Showerhead
- ☐ Skateboard
- ☐ Skulls (2)
- ☐ Skunk
- ☐ Sock
- ☐ Star
- ☐ Swing
- ☐ Top hat
- ☐ Trash can
- ☐ Trumpet
- ☐ Umbrellas (2)
- ☐ Wagon

Next to the dungeon are the wildest lanes in town. It's a great place to do anything—but bowl!

FIND FREDDIE & LISA AT THE GHOSTLY BOWLING ALLEY AND...

- ☐ Arrow
- ☐ Balloon
- ☐ Bat
- ☐ Bird
- ☐ Bodiless head
- ☐ Bomb
- ☐ Boom box
- ☐ Broken ball
- ☐ Broom
- ☐ Cactus
- ☐ Candles (2)
- ☐ Carrot
- ☐ Delivery creature
- ☐ Dog
- ☐ Earphones
- ☐ Flower
- ☐ Hamburger
- ☐ Hot dog
- ☐ Humpty Dumpty
- ☐ Mouse
- ☐ Mummy
- ☐ Mummy's ball
- ☐ Orange
- ☐ Pear
- ☐ Pennant
- ☐ Periscope
- ☐ Rabbit
- ☐ Robot
- ☐ Sailboat
- ☐ Skull
- ☐ Snowman
- ☐ Spring
- ☐ Square ball
- ☐ Sunglasses (2 pairs)
- ☐ Sword
- ☐ Tennis racket
- ☐ Tombstone
- ☐ Watermelon slice
- ☐ Who quit?
- ☐ Who ordered pizza?
- ☐ Worm
- ☐ Yo-yo

Dr. Frankenstein has lots of patients who need lots of patience.

FIND FREDDIE & LISA IN DR. FRANKENSTEIN'S LABORATORY AND...

- ☐ Black cat
- ☐ Book
- ☐ Bow tie
- ☐ Bride
- ☐ Bunny fiend
- ☐ Candle
- ☐ Cheese
- ☐ Dog
- ☐ Dracula
- ☐ Duck
- ☐ Feather
- ☐ Greeting card
- ☐ Hot hat
- ☐ Ice-cream pop
- ☐ Invisible person
- ☐ Neckerchief
- ☐ Paintbrush
- ☐ Paint bucket
- ☐ Pickax
- ☐ Roller skates
- ☐ Sailor fiend
- ☐ Saw
- ☐ Screwdriver
- ☐ Shovel
- ☐ Skull
- ☐ Suspenders
- ☐ Thing-in-a-sack
- ☐ Three-eyed creature
- ☐ Three-legged thing
- ☐ Toothbrush
- ☐ Tulip
- ☐ TV set
- ☐ Two-headed thing
- ☐ Watch
- ☐ Who has a sore throat?
- ☐ Who has a toothache?
- ☐ Who needs a haircut?
- ☐ Who snores?
- ☐ Who's been shrunk?
- ☐ Who's on a diet?
- ☐ Wooden block

After dinner, Freddie and Lisa explore a junk-filled room upstairs. There they find someone who <u>really</u> knows how to save!

FIND FREDDIE & LISA IN DRACULA'S ATTIC AND...

- ☐ Book
- ☐ Boomerang
- ☐ Broom
- ☐ Calendar
- ☐ Candy cane
- ☐ Chef's hat
- ☐ Clocks (2)
- ☐ Cracked mirror
- ☐ Fire hydrant
- ☐ Garden hose
- ☐ Golf club
- ☐ Ice-cream cone
- ☐ Key
- ☐ Moon
- ☐ Mouse
- ☐ Necklace
- ☐ Necktie
- ☐ Oar
- ☐ Old-fashioned radio
- ☐ Paint bucket
- ☐ Paper airplane
- ☐ Pencil
- ☐ Pyramid
- ☐ Santa's hat
- ☐ Saw
- ☐ Skateboard
- ☐ Skulls (4)
- ☐ Slice of pizza
- ☐ Spray can
- ☐ Stocking
- ☐ Straw
- ☐ String of pearls
- ☐ Stuffed panda
- ☐ Target
- ☐ Telephone booth
- ☐ Top hat
- ☐ Train engine
- ☐ Viking helmet
- ☐ Wagon wheel
- ☐ Wig
- ☐ Yarn

The monsters walk very carefully when they visit this room!

FIND FREDDIE & LISA IN THE COBWEB ROOM AND...

- ☐ Baby carriage
- ☐ Bats (2)
- ☐ Binoculars
- ☐ Boot
- ☐ Bow tie
- ☐ Boxing glove
- ☐ Broom
- ☐ Cup
- ☐ Dog
- ☐ Duck
- ☐ Earring
- ☐ Electric plug
- ☐ Fish
- ☐ Flower
- ☐ Football helmet
- ☐ Fork
- ☐ Ghosts (2)
- ☐ Hammer
- ☐ Heart
- ☐ Key
- ☐ Kite
- ☐ Lock
- ☐ Moon face
- ☐ Mummy
- ☐ Number 13
- ☐ Old-fashioned radio
- ☐ Paintbrush
- ☐ Pencil
- ☐ Ring
- ☐ Robot
- ☐ Screwdriver
- ☐ Ship
- ☐ Six-fingered creature
- ☐ Skull
- ☐ Spider
- ☐ Top hat
- ☐ Train engine
- ☐ Turtles (2)
- ☐ Umbrella
- ☐ Wagon

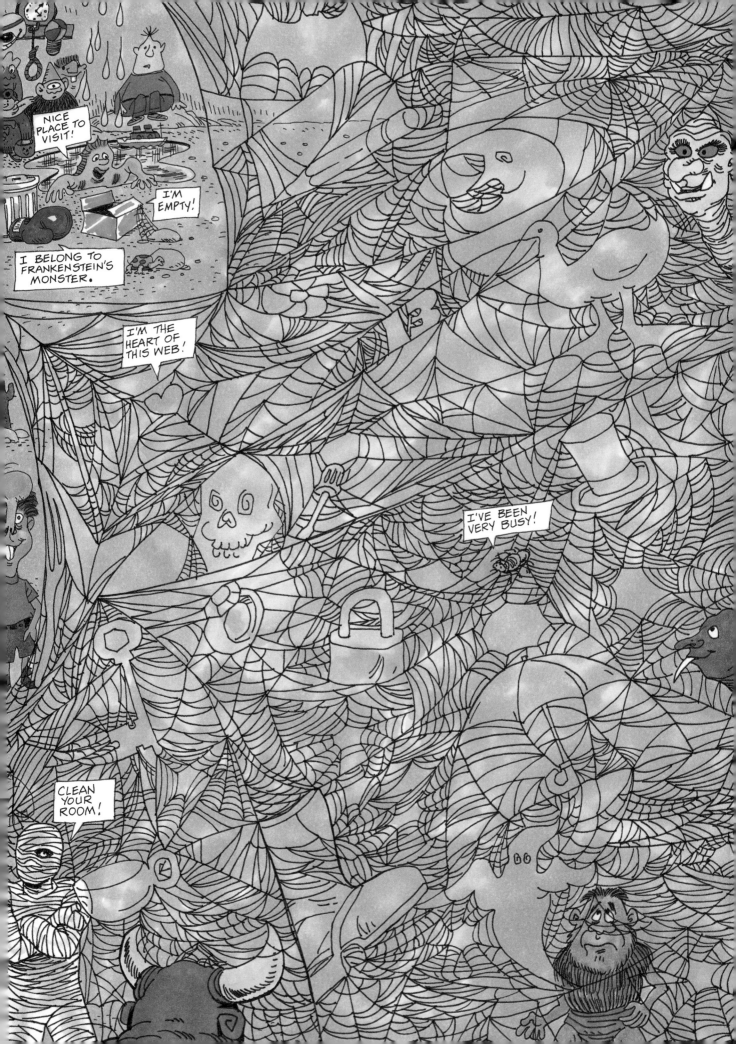

FIND FREDDIE & LISA IN THE MONSTERS' PLAYROOM AND...

- ☐ Artist
- ☐ Balloon
- ☐ Banana peel
- ☐ Barbell
- ☐ Beanie
- ☐ Birds (2)
- ☐ Blackboard
- ☐ Crayons (5)
- ☐ Donkey
- ☐ Fish
- ☐ Football
- ☐ Haunted house
- ☐ Hole in the head
- ☐ Hood
- ☐ Ice skate
- ☐ Jack-o'-lanterns (4)
- ☐ Jacks (4)
- ☐ Joke book
- ☐ Juggler
- ☐ Loose change
- ☐ Mask
- ☐ Monster-in-the-box
- ☐ Monster puppet
- ☐ Mummy doll
- ☐ Musician
- ☐ Nail
- ☐ Pail
- ☐ "Pin-the-tail-on-the-donkey"
- ☐ Pogo stick
- ☐ Rubber ducky
- ☐ Sailboat
- ☐ Snake
- ☐ Telephone
- ☐ Tepee
- ☐ Three-legged thing
- ☐ Tricycle
- ☐ Truck
- ☐ Turtle
- ☐ TV set
- ☐ Who attends "Horror U"?
- ☐ Wind-up monster

It's time for Freddie & Lisa to go. The friendly monsters hope their new friends will return soon.

FIND FREDDIE & LISA LEAVING THE HAUNTED HOUSE AND...

- ☐ Apple
- ☐ Arrow
- ☐ Balloon
- ☐ Birds (2)
- ☐ Box
- ☐ Broken heart
- ☐ Brooms (2)
- ☐ Candles (2)
- ☐ Clock
- ☐ Crown
- ☐ Did they have fun?
- ☐ Dog
- ☐ Duck
- ☐ Envelope
- ☐ Feather
- ☐ Firecracker
- ☐ Flower
- ☐ Ice skates
- ☐ Jack-o'-lanterns (4)
- ☐ Key
- ☐ Ladder
- ☐ Lamp
- ☐ Moon face
- ☐ Mouse
- ☐ Painted egg
- ☐ Periscope
- ☐ Rabbit
- ☐ Roller skates
- ☐ Scarves (3)
- ☐ Seven-fingered creature
- ☐ Shovel
- ☐ Skull
- ☐ Straw
- ☐ Tick-Tack-Toe
- ☐ Top hat
- ☐ Tree
- ☐ TV camera
- ☐ Umbrella
- ☐ When will they return?
- ☐ Which exit did they use?
- ☐ Who will miss them the most?
- ☐ Who doesn't use toothpaste?

Freddie and Lisa are
here with a few of their
playmates.

Donald	Hector
Frankie	Susie
Laura	Bunny Honey
Sam	Santa
Santa's helpers — Fee, Fi, Fo and Fun	

MONSTER MADNESS

There once was an ancient house, in an ancient part of town, that was discovered by two not so ancient children. They wanted to go inside, but first they had to find the following hidden pictures. Can you help them?

☐ Banana
☐ Bone
☐ Book
☐ Boot
☐ Bottle
☐ Broom
☐ Carrot
☐ Elephant
☐ Envelope
☐ Fish
☐ Flower
☐ Flying bat
☐ Fork
☐ Guitar

☐ Hairbrush
☐ Hammer
☐ Heart
☐ Hockey stick
☐ Horseshoe
☐ Hot dog
☐ Kitchen knife
☐ Lost wallet
☐ Owl
☐ Palm tree
☐ Pencil
☐ Question mark

☐ Rabbit
☐ Sailboat
☐ Saw
☐ Screwdriver
☐ Skull
☐ Snake
☐ Star
☐ Tepee
☐ Tick-tack-toe
☐ Toothbrush
☐ Top hat
☐ Zipper

WELCOME TO ANCIENT ACRES

WE FOUND IT! LET'S GO INSIDE!

NOT FOR SALE

In the ancient house, was an ancient truck, which was opened with an ancient key, by the not so ancient children. Out of the trunk came many strange things including the hidden objects below.

☐ Arrow
☐ Balloon
☐ Bearded man
☐ Carrot
☐ Chicken
☐ Clown
☐ Cow
☐ Elephant
☐ Envelope
☐ Fish

☐ Giraffe
☐ Horse
☐ Kite
☐ Moon face
☐ Mouse
☐ Pumpkin
☐ Rabbit
☐ Saw

☐ Snowman
☐ Tepee
☐ Tombstone
☐ Turtle
☐ Unicorn
☐ Watermelon slice
☐ Witch

Did you ever see such a sight in your life? No, it's not three blind mice—it's monsters, monsters, monsters! Monsters can be found everywhere along with the following hidden pictures. Can you find them all?

☐ Arrow
☐ Automobile
☐ Bell
☐ Bird
☐ Candle
☐ Candy canes (2)
☐ Clothespin
☐ Comb
☐ Drum
☐ Evergreen tree
☐ Fish
☐ Flower
☐ Football
☐ Fork

☐ Hairbrush
☐ Hot dog
☐ Kangaroo
☐ Key
☐ Locket
☐ Mouse
☐ Pen
☐ Pencil
☐ Scarf
☐ Skateboard
☐ Sock
☐ Star
☐ Tent
☐ Turtle
☐ Umbrella

In another ancient room in the ancient house the two kids found ... an
ANCIENT FAMILY ALBUM! Whose pictures do you think were inside?
Wait! Before you can open it, you must first find:

- Arrow
- Banana
- Bear
- Cactus
- Cane
- Cat
- Deer
- Duck
- Fork
- Frog
- Ghost
- Giraffe
- Goat
- Heart
- Hot dog
- Ice-cream cone

- Lamb
- Monkey
- Mouse
- Owl
- Pencil
- Pig
- Rabbit
- Ring
- Rooster
- Saw
- Skull
- Snake
- Squirrel
- Star
- Turtle

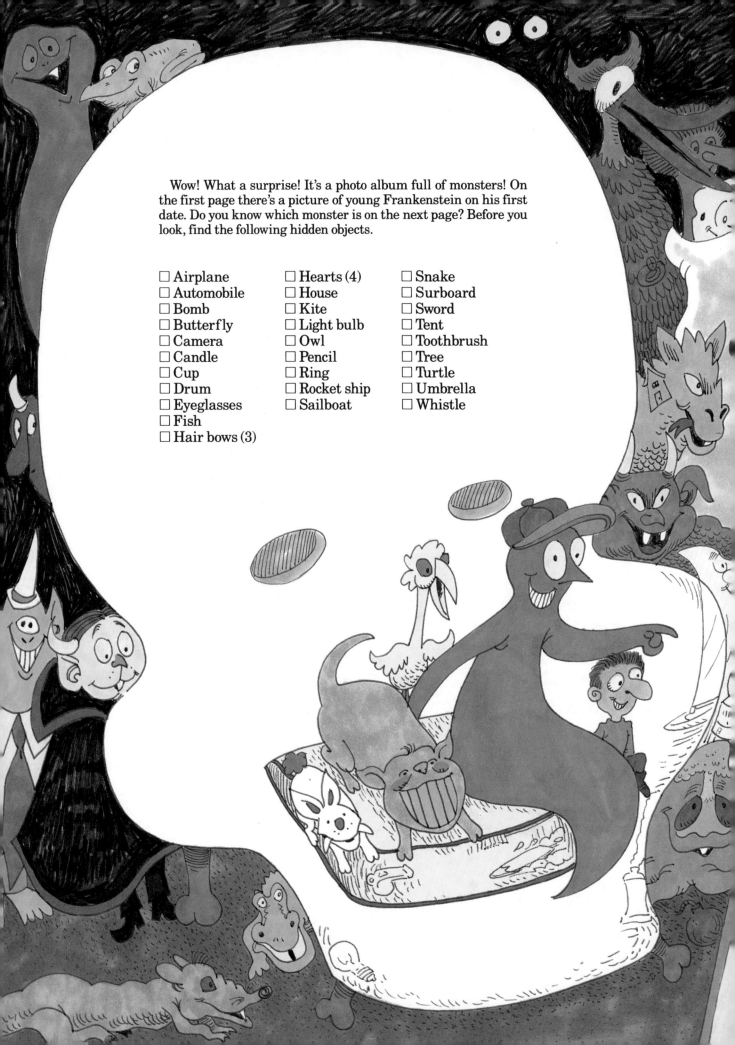

Wow! What a surprise! It's a photo album full of monsters! On the first page there's a picture of young Frankenstein on his first date. Do you know which monster is on the next page? Before you look, find the following hidden objects.

- ☐ Airplane
- ☐ Automobile
- ☐ Bomb
- ☐ Butterfly
- ☐ Camera
- ☐ Candle
- ☐ Cup
- ☐ Drum
- ☐ Eyeglasses
- ☐ Fish
- ☐ Hair bows (3)

- ☐ Hearts (4)
- ☐ House
- ☐ Kite
- ☐ Light bulb
- ☐ Owl
- ☐ Pencil
- ☐ Ring
- ☐ Rocket ship
- ☐ Sailboat

- ☐ Snake
- ☐ Surboard
- ☐ Sword
- ☐ Tent
- ☐ Toothbrush
- ☐ Tree
- ☐ Turtle
- ☐ Umbrella
- ☐ Whistle

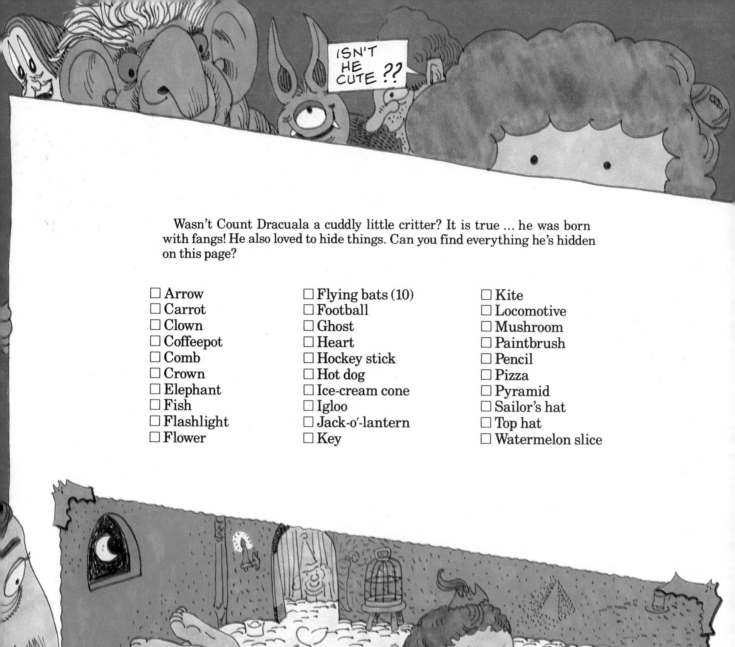

Wasn't Count Dracuala a cuddly little critter? It is true ... he was born with fangs! He also loved to hide things. Can you find everything he's hidden on this page?

- ☐ Arrow
- ☐ Carrot
- ☐ Clown
- ☐ Coffeepot
- ☐ Comb
- ☐ Crown
- ☐ Elephant
- ☐ Fish
- ☐ Flashlight
- ☐ Flower

- ☐ Flying bats (10)
- ☐ Football
- ☐ Ghost
- ☐ Heart
- ☐ Hockey stick
- ☐ Hot dog
- ☐ Ice-cream cone
- ☐ Igloo
- ☐ Jack-o'-lantern
- ☐ Key

- ☐ Kite
- ☐ Locomotive
- ☐ Mushroom
- ☐ Paintbrush
- ☐ Pencil
- ☐ Pizza
- ☐ Pyramid
- ☐ Sailor's hat
- ☐ Top hat
- ☐ Watermelon slice

This page has the largest picture in the monster family album. It's the abominable snow-kid building snow monsters. He's also thrown in some hidden pictures. Look closely to see if you can find them all.

☐ Alligator
☐ Banana
☐ Basket
☐ Bow tie
☐ Bowling ball
☐ Cactus
☐ Can
☐ Candle
☐ Candy cane
☐ Chair
☐ Cheese
☐ Chef's hat
☐ Cowboy hat
☐ Duck
☐ Fish
☐ Ghost
☐ Heart
☐ Hot dog
☐ Ice skate
☐ Ice-cream cone
☐ Ladder
☐ Lamp
☐ Lion
☐ Mouse
☐ Paintbrush
☐ Picture frame
☐ Pie
☐ Pig
☐ Pirate
☐ Shoe
☐ Shovel
☐ Top hat
☐ Umbrella
☐ Watering can
☐ Witch

Here's the mummy showing off his childhood pictures. You can certainly get wrapped up in them! You can also get wrapped up in looking for the following hidden objects.

- ☐ Apple
- ☐ Arrow
- ☐ Artist
- ☐ Bird
- ☐ Blimp
- ☐ Bone
- ☐ Book
- ☐ Broom
- ☐ Clothespin
- ☐ Cupcake
- ☐ Drum
- ☐ Envelope

- ☐ Fish
- ☐ Flying bat
- ☐ Football
- ☐ Ghost
- ☐ Golf club
- ☐ Hammer
- ☐ Kangaroo
- ☐ Kite
- ☐ Magnifying glass

- ☐ Owl
- ☐ Paintbrush
- ☐ Pinocchio
- ☐ Quarter moon
- ☐ Sailor's hat
- ☐ Saw
- ☐ Scarecrow
- ☐ Wagon

These are really terrific pictures ... the best in the album! They are, of course, pictures of the invisible man throughout the years. He is looking with you to find:

- ☐ Banana
- ☐ Basket
- ☐ Bone
- ☐ Candy cane
- ☐ Carrot
- ☐ Cheese
- ☐ Cupcake
- ☐ Evergreen tree
- ☐ Fire hydrant
- ☐ Football
- ☐ Graduation cap
- ☐ Guitar
- ☐ Hamburger
- ☐ Heart
- ☐ Hot dog
- ☐ Ice-cream soda
- ☐ Light bulb
- ☐ Monster-in-a-box
- ☐ Mouse
- ☐ Pear
- ☐ Pencil
- ☐ Rose
- ☐ Screwdriver
- ☐ Shovel
- ☐ Snail
- ☐ Star
- ☐ Tent
- ☐ Turtle
- ☐ TV set
- ☐ Unicorn

FIRST BIRTHDAY ↵

KID LEAGUE STAR ↵

FIRST DAY OF SCHOOL ↵

INVISIBLE PAPER ↵

SCHOOL FIELD TRIP ⤴

SOCCER CHAMP ⤴

TALKING TO SANTA ⤴

FIRST INVISIBLE MAN ON THE MOON ⤴

One picture is too big to fit in the album.
It's so big, it's hiding:

- [ ] Balloons (2)
- [ ] Bats (2)
- [ ] Birdhouse
- [ ] Birds (2)
- [ ] Boat
- [ ] Clock
- [ ] Coffeepot
- [ ] Covered wagon
- [ ] Crown
- [ ] Cup
- [ ] Dog
- [ ] Elephant
- [ ] Feather
- [ ] Fish (3)
- [ ] Fork
- [ ] Hearts (2)
- [ ] Horseshoe
- [ ] Jack-o'-lantern
- [ ] Jump rope
- [ ] Key
- [ ] Kite
- [ ] Mailbox
- [ ] Mermaid
- [ ] Old radio
- [ ] Old sock
- [ ] Old tire
- [ ] Pizza
- [ ] Tepee
- [ ] Worm

A MONSTER FAMILY PICNIC.

The monsters were so happy to have shared their ANCIENT FAMILY ALBUM with the kids, they asked the children to pose with them for a group photograph. However, before the picture can be taken, you must find:

☐ Bird's nest
☐ Bow tie
☐ Boxing glove
☐ Butterfly
☐ Camel
☐ Cow
☐ Crayon
☐ Deflated balloon
☐ Dinosaur
☐ Eight ball
☐ Elephant

☐ False teeth
☐ Fish
☐ Flying bat
☐ Football
☐ Football helmet
☐ Hamburger
☐ Hammer
☐ Igloo
☐ Kite
☐ Locomotive
☐ Model plane
☐ Mouse

☐ Music note
☐ Paintbrush
☐ Sled
☐ Slice of pizza
☐ Snake
☐ Tent
☐ Thermometer
☐ Top hat
☐ Wind-up car

Early one morning, Frankie has a brilliant idea. He thinks it would be great fun to visit some old friends he hasn't seen in a long time.

FIND FRANKIE
IN HIS NUTTY
NEIGHBORHOOD
AND...

☐ Book
☐ Bowling ball
☐ Bucket
☐ Candle
☐ Dog
☐ Duck
☐ Fish (3)
☐ Flying bats (3)
☐ Football helmet
☐ Hammer
☐ Heart
☐ Jack-o'-lantern
☐ Moose head
☐ Periscope
☐ Pick
☐ Pinocchio
☐ Rain slicker
☐ Roller skates
☐ Sailor hat
☐ Scarecrow
☐ Skier
☐ Skull
☐ Snow shovel
☐ Star
☐ Tepee
☐ Thermometer
☐ Tulip
☐ Turtle
☐ Watering can
☐ Wreath

Frankie first looks for his old, old friend Manny Mummy in a place with lots of sand.

FIND MANNY MUMMY IN THE DRY DESERT AND…

- ☐ Balloons (3)
- ☐ Banana peel
- ☐ Bathtub
- ☐ Birdhouse
- ☐ Brooms (2)
- ☐ Earring
- ☐ Fire hydrant
- ☐ Fish (2)
- ☐ Flower
- ☐ Gas pump
- ☐ Ring
- ☐ Sailor hat
- ☐ Sand castle
- ☐ Sand pail
- ☐ Sled
- ☐ Slingshot
- ☐ Snake
- ☐ Snowman
- ☐ Soccer ball
- ☐ Star
- ☐ Straw
- ☐ Suitcase
- ☐ Surfboard
- ☐ Turtle
- ☐ TV antenna
- ☐ Umbrella
- ☐ Watering can
- ☐ Watermelon slice

Frankie and Manny Mummy set off to find their friend Batty Bat. He lives in a strange little town.

FIND BATTY BAT IN TERRIFYING TRANSYLVANIA AND...

☐ Alligator
☐ Arrows (2)
☐ Baker
☐ Bomb
☐ Bones (6)
☐ Book
☐ Bride and groom
☐ Broken heart
☐ Broken mirror
☐ Candle
☐ Dog
☐ Fish
☐ Flower
☐ Football
☐ Fortune teller
☐ Hair dryer
☐ Kite
☐ Lion
☐ Mouse
☐ Nail
☐ Octopus
☐ Rabbit
☐ Scissors
☐ Skulls (4)
☐ Top hat
☐ Training wheels
☐ Umbrella
☐ Vulture
☐ Wind-up monster
☐ Worm

Now they are off to find another old pal. This one lives in the heart of a swamp!

FIND SWAMPY SAM IN THIS MUSHY MARSH AND...

☐ Apple
☐ Barber pole
☐ Cupcake
☐ Drum
☐ Fish (5)
☐ Football helmet
☐ Fork
☐ Frog
☐ Grand piano
☐ Hammer
☐ Key
☐ Lost boot
☐ Lost mitten
☐ Medal
☐ Moon face
☐ Necktie
☐ Palm tree
☐ Pencil
☐ Pizza slice
☐ Ring
☐ Snake
☐ Soccer ball
☐ Sock
☐ Speaker
☐ Spoon
☐ Tent
☐ Toothbrush
☐ Trumpet
☐ Umbrellas (2)

Warren Werewolf is Frankie's next friend to find. He plays baseball with the Dead End Dodgers.

FIND WARREN WEREWOLF AT THIS BUMBLING BALLPARK AND…

- ☐ Bicycle horn
- ☐ Bone
- ☐ Cactus
- ☐ Camera
- ☐ Candy cane
- ☐ Carrot
- ☐ Cookie
- ☐ Crown
- ☐ Duck
- ☐ Empty can
- ☐ Eyeglasses (2)
- ☐ Feather
- ☐ Fir tree
- ☐ Flamingo
- ☐ Footprint
- ☐ Frog
- ☐ Heart
- ☐ Horseshoe
- ☐ Humpty Dumpty
- ☐ Kite
- ☐ Lamp
- ☐ Mouse
- ☐ Pliers
- ☐ Sewing needle
- ☐ Six-fingered glove
- ☐ Skull
- ☐ Squirrel
- ☐ Tick-tack-toe
- ☐ Whistle
- ☐ Witch
- ☐ Worm

Frankie and his pals go to an old schoolhouse where their friend Lena Lightning is a student.

FIND LENA LIGHTNING AMONGST HER CREEPY CLASSMATES AND...

☐ Apple core
☐ Bandage
☐ Bell
☐ Bone tree
☐ Broken mirror
☐ Cactus
☐ Candles (3)
☐ Crystal ball
☐ Egg
☐ Firecracker
☐ Flashlight
☐ Flying bats (3)
☐ Fortune teller
☐ Heart
☐ Hot dog
☐ Ice skate
☐ Mask
☐ Mouse
☐ Necktie
☐ Owl
☐ Pencil
☐ Pick
☐ Puss-in-boot
☐ Saw
☐ Shark fin
☐ Skateboard
☐ Skunk
☐ Snakes (2)
☐ Star
☐ Vulture
☐ Worm

Next, Frankie and his friends set out to visit Greta Ghost, but none of her neighbors have seen her in a while.

FIND FRANKIE AND HIS OTHER FRIENDS AT GRETA'S HAUNTED HOUSE AND…

- ☐ Alligator
- ☐ Arrows (2)
- ☐ Axe
- ☐ Balloons (5)
- ☐ Banana peel
- ☐ Bowling ball
- ☐ Broom
- ☐ Cup
- ☐ Dart
- ☐ Drum
- ☐ Flying bats (3)
- ☐ Fork
- ☐ Hammer
- ☐ Hatched egg
- ☐ Heart
- ☐ Keys (2)
- ☐ Ring
- ☐ Screwdriver
- ☐ Ski
- ☐ Skull and crossbones
- ☐ Stool
- ☐ Sword
- ☐ Teapot
- ☐ Tepee
- ☐ Torn sock
- ☐ Turtle
- ☐ Umbrella
- ☐ Water bucket
- ☐ Windsock
- ☐ Wreath

Frankie can't find Greta Ghost at the haunted house, so he and the others check the new condos and find her haunting there.

FIND GRETA GHOST IN MODERN MONSTERVILLE AND...

☐ Arrow
☐ Balloons (4)
☐ Bones (2)
☐ Cactus
☐ Camel
☐ Candles (3)
☐ Fire hydrant
☐ Firecracker
☐ Fish (3)
☐ Flowers (3)
☐ Football helmet
☐ Four-armed
    monster
☐ Frog
☐ Hoe
☐ Horseshoe
☐ Ice-cream cone
☐ Igloo
☐ Kites (2)
☐ Lollipop
☐ Lost bathing
    trunks
☐ Lost boot
☐ Mice (3)
☐ Painted egg
☐ Periscope
☐ Pyramid
☐ Quarter moon
☐ Rabbit
☐ Roller skates
☐ Seahorse
☐ Seal
☐ Sunglasses (2)
☐ Surfboard

Together at last, they all go on a picnic...where else but in a cemetery!

FIND FRANKIE AND HIS FRIENDS IN THIS GHOULISH GRAVEYARD AND...

- ☐ Apron
- ☐ Baseball cap
- ☐ Broom
- ☐ Burned-out candle
- ☐ Chef's hat
- ☐ Clothespin
- ☐ Crayon
- ☐ Crown
- ☐ Fish (2)
- ☐ Flower
- ☐ Fork
- ☐ Guitar
- ☐ Heart
- ☐ Hockey stick
- ☐ House
- ☐ Light bulb
- ☐ Mice (2)
- ☐ Paintbrush
- ☐ Picture frame
- ☐ Pig
- ☐ Ring
- ☐ Shovel
- ☐ Sock
- ☐ Spoon
- ☐ Straw
- ☐ Submarine
- ☐ Truck
- ☐ TV antenna
- ☐ Worm
- ☐ Wristwatch

After the picnic, Frankie and his friends go to see…you guessed it… a monster movie.

FIND FRANKIE AND HIS FRIENDS AT THIS FRIGHTENING FLICK AND…

- ☐ Apple core
- ☐ Arrow
- ☐ Clothespin
- ☐ Clown
- ☐ Dog
- ☐ Drum
- ☐ Eight ball
- ☐ Eyeglasses
- ☐ Faucet
- ☐ Fish skeleton
- ☐ Flashlight
- ☐ Football player
- ☐ Fortune teller
- ☐ Heart
- ☐ Ice-cream pop
- ☐ Moon faces (2)
- ☐ Necktie
- ☐ Oilcan
- ☐ Paper airplane
- ☐ Periscope
- ☐ Piggy bank
- ☐ Rabbit
- ☐ Roller skates
- ☐ Sailboat
- ☐ Skunk
- ☐ Star
- ☐ Superhero
- ☐ Top hat
- ☐ Trash can
- ☐ Trumpet
- ☐ Worm

While walking back from the movie Frankie and his friends see a frightening sight!

FIND FRANKIE AND HIS FRIENDS WITH THESE TERRIFIC TRICK-OR-TREATERS AND…

- ☐ Balloon
- ☐ Big lips
- ☐ Broom
- ☐ Butterfly
- ☐ Candy cane
- ☐ Carrot
- ☐ Chef's hat
- ☐ Crown
- ☐ Drumstick
- ☐ Earmuffs
- ☐ Envelope
- ☐ Fish
- ☐ Fork
- ☐ Key
- ☐ Lost sneaker
- ☐ Moustache
- ☐ Paintbrush
- ☐ Paper bag
- ☐ Pencil
- ☐ Pizza
- ☐ Roller skates
- ☐ Sailor hat
- ☐ Shovel
- ☐ Sock
- ☐ Squirrel
- ☐ Star
- ☐ Top hat
- ☐ Tree ornament
- ☐ Umbrella
- ☐ Watering can
- ☐ Worm

It's time for Frankie and friends to say goodbye… for now that is. They've planned to get together real soon and you're invited to join in the fun!

FIND FRANKIE,
MANNY MUMMY,
BATTY BAT,
SWAMPY SAM,
WARREN
WEREWOLF, LENA
LIGHTNING, GRETA
GHOST AND…

☐ Apple core
☐ Arrow
☐ Baseball
☐ Bone
☐ Crayon
☐ Flowerpot
☐ Frog
☐ Heart

☐ Ice-cream cone
☐ Kite
☐ Owl
☐ Turtle
☐ Watermelon slice
☐ Worm
…and lots of
other things.

Welcome to Creepy Castle, the castle that was never built. One moonless, creepy night it just appeared! Enter at your own risk! But first, find the following things hidden in this picture.

☐ Airplane
☐ Anchor
☐ Automobile
☐ Axe
☐ Bottle
☐ Broom
☐ Chair
☐ Clown's face
☐ Coffeepot
☐ Cup

☐ Duck
☐ Fire hydrant
☐ Fish
☐ Football
☐ Fork
☐ Hammer
☐ Heart
☐ Hockey stick
☐ Ice-cream cone
☐ Key

☐ Kite
☐ Paintbrush
☐ Pencil
☐ Ring
☐ Sailboat
☐ Screwdriver
☐ Star
☐ Toothbrush

WELCOME?

Racing through a partly open curtain, our friends enter the room of a famous monster star who's hidden all kinds of things. Can you find them?

☐ Automobile
☐ Axe
☐ Basket
☐ Bat
☐ Bird
☐ Bone
☐ Candle
☐ Cups (2)
☐ Elephant
☐ Fish
☐ Flower
☐ Guitar
☐ Hammer
☐ Heart
☐ Igloo
☐ Kangaroo
☐ Mermaid
☐ Mitten
☐ Moon face
☐ Mouse
☐ Party hat
☐ Pencil
☐ Rabbit
☐ Sailboat
☐ Star
☐ Toothbrush
☐ Tugboat
☐ Whale

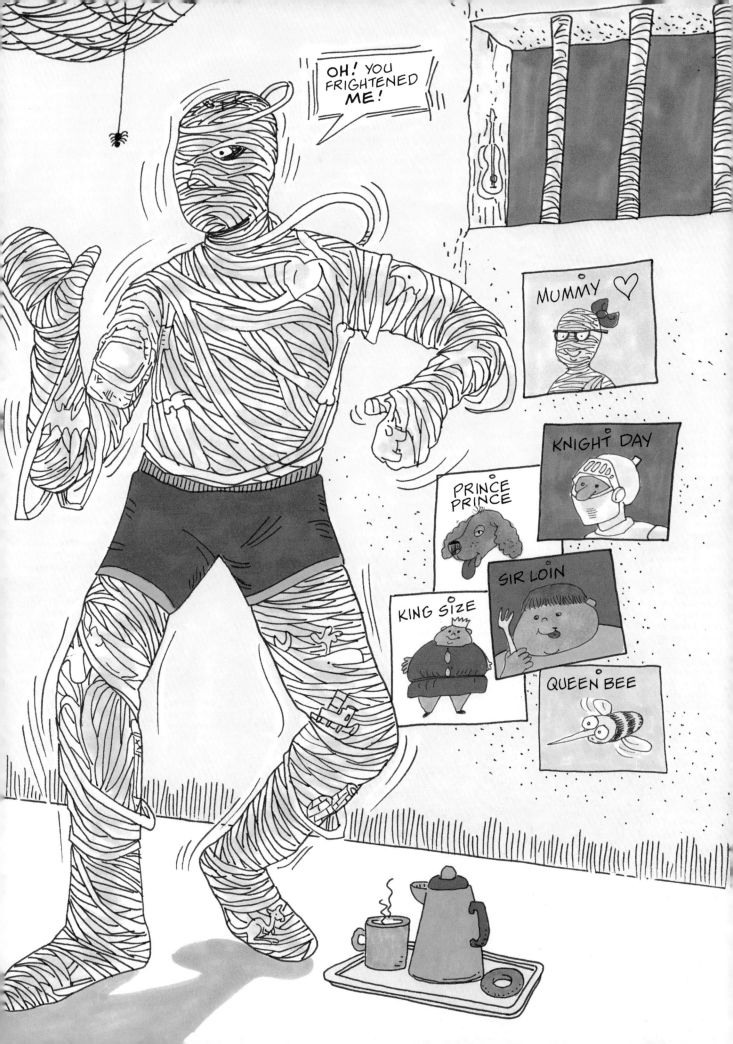

Now there's a weird sight — a headless knight! Could he be related to the headless horseman of Sleepy Hollow?
Before going on, find these hidden pictures.

- ☐ Baseball bat
- ☐ Book
- ☐ Bottle
- ☐ Chicken
- ☐ Cow's head
- ☐ Cupcake
- ☐ Duck
- ☐ Eagle's head
- ☐ Ear of corn
- ☐ Envelope
- ☐ Feather
- ☐ Fish
- ☐ Fishhook
- ☐ Frog
- ☐ Ghost
- ☐ Hot dog
- ☐ Key
- ☐ Paper clip
- ☐ Pea pod
- ☐ Saw
- ☐ Shoe
- ☐ Slice of bread
- ☐ Sock
- ☐ Toothbrush
- ☐ Turtle
- ☐ Umbrella
- ☐ Wheelbarrow

What lurks beneath this new knight's hood? Is he a handsome hero or another creepy creature? Before you turn the page to find out, look for the following hidden pictures.

☐ Arrow
☐ Astronaut
☐ Banana
☐ Brush
☐ Cactus
☐ Carrot
☐ Crab
☐ Electric guitar
☐ Fish

☐ Heart
☐ Helicopter
☐ Hot dog
☐ Ice-cream cone
☐ Invisible knight
☐ Key
☐ Kite
☐ Magnet
☐ Parachute

☐ Pelican
☐ Rocket ship
☐ Sailboat
☐ Skis
☐ Star
☐ Teapot
☐ Toothbrush
☐ Truck
☐ Turtle

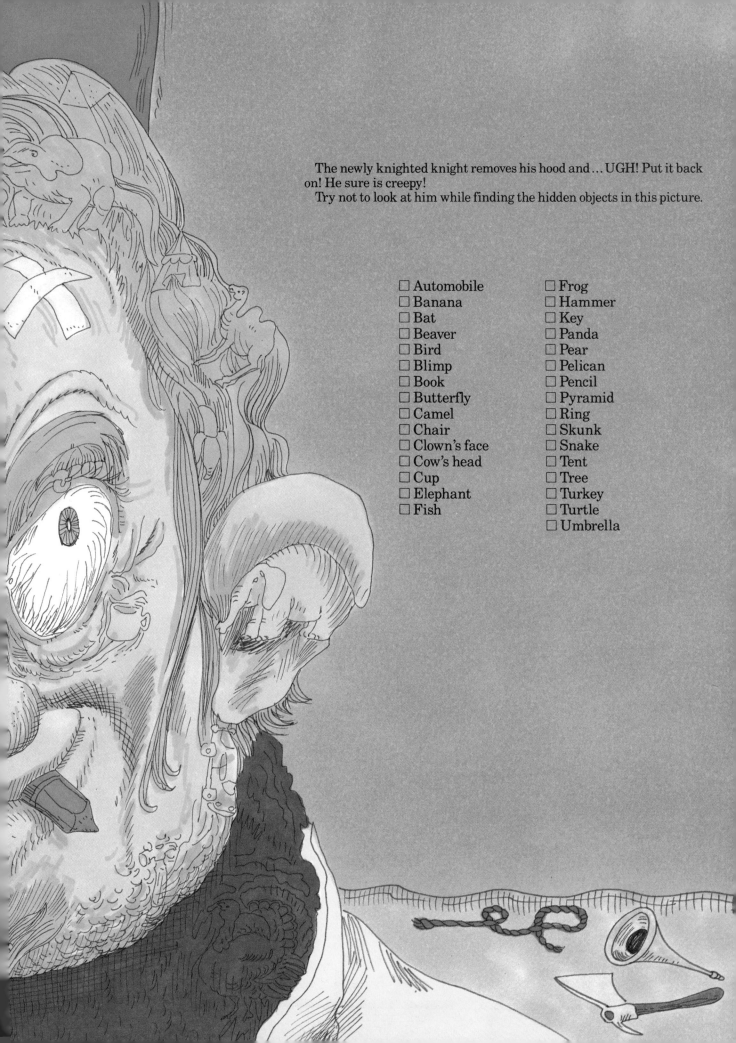

The newly knighted knight removes his hood and ... UGH! Put it back
on! He sure is creepy!
Try not to look at him while finding the hidden objects in this picture.

☐ Automobile
☐ Banana
☐ Bat
☐ Beaver
☐ Bird
☐ Blimp
☐ Book
☐ Butterfly
☐ Camel
☐ Chair
☐ Clown's face
☐ Cow's head
☐ Cup
☐ Elephant
☐ Fish

☐ Frog
☐ Hammer
☐ Key
☐ Panda
☐ Pear
☐ Pelican
☐ Pencil
☐ Pyramid
☐ Ring
☐ Skunk
☐ Snake
☐ Tent
☐ Tree
☐ Turkey
☐ Turtle
☐ Umbrella

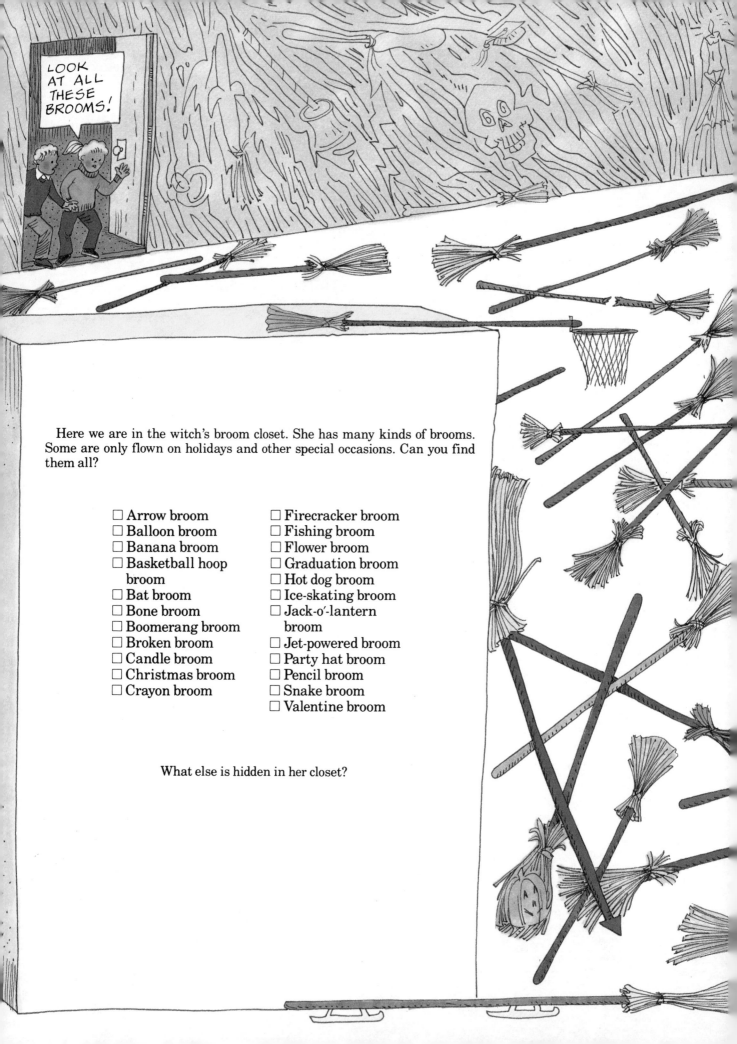

LOOK AT ALL THESE BROOMS!

Here we are in the witch's broom closet. She has many kinds of brooms. Some are only flown on holidays and other special occasions. Can you find them all?

☐ Arrow broom
☐ Balloon broom
☐ Banana broom
☐ Basketball hoop broom
☐ Bat broom
☐ Bone broom
☐ Boomerang broom
☐ Broken broom
☐ Candle broom
☐ Christmas broom
☐ Crayon broom

☐ Firecracker broom
☐ Fishing broom
☐ Flower broom
☐ Graduation broom
☐ Hot dog broom
☐ Ice-skating broom
☐ Jack-o'-lantern broom
☐ Jet-powered broom
☐ Party hat broom
☐ Pencil broom
☐ Snake broom
☐ Valentine broom

What else is hidden in her closet?

Through a hole in the wall, our friends take a peek at Wizard Merlin the magician, as he creates nasty nightmares.

Peek carefully at this picture and find the following hidden objects.

- ☐ Airplane
- ☐ Apple
- ☐ Arrow
- ☐ Axe
- ☐ Bat
- ☐ Drum
- ☐ Elephant's head
- ☐ Football
- ☐ Ghost
- ☐ Gorilla

- ☐ Hearts (3)
- ☐ Helicopter
- ☐ Horse's head
- ☐ Ice-cream cone
- ☐ Kite
- ☐ Lion's face
- ☐ Lizard
- ☐ Magnet
- ☐ Mask
- ☐ Mouse

- ☐ Mushroom
- ☐ Octopus
- ☐ Owl
- ☐ Paintbrush
- ☐ Shark
- ☐ Skull
- ☐ Snake
- ☐ Top hat
- ☐ Toucan
- ☐ Windmill

Surprise! Our fearless friends have been invited to a party in their honor. Looks like they're having a creepy, crazy good time!

You too can join in on the fun by finding the following hidden pictures.

- ☐ Arrows (2)
- ☐ Bat
- ☐ Bottle
- ☐ Cup
- ☐ Fish
- ☐ Flower
- ☐ Fork
- ☐ Ghosts (2)
- ☐ Hot dog
- ☐ Ice skate
- ☐ Key
- ☐ Kite
- ☐ Light bulb
- ☐ Mitten
- ☐ Music note

- ☐ Paintbrush
- ☐ Pencil
- ☐ Penguin
- ☐ Piggy bank
- ☐ Pinwheel
- ☐ Rocket
- ☐ Rocking chair
- ☐ Roller skate
- ☐ Seal
- ☐ Snake
- ☐ Sock
- ☐ Spoon
- ☐ Star
- ☐ Toothbrush
- ☐ Truck
- ☐ Umbrella

I WAS CROWNED PRINCE!

Congratulations! You have survived Creepy Castle! But what crazy gifts have our friends brought home?
See if you can find these peculiar presents. They are hidden in the picture below.

☐ Barbell
☐ Broken clock
☐ Cactus
☐ Cat
☐ Dog
☐ Fire hydrant
☐ Flying bat

☐ Fountain
☐ Heart
☐ Ice-cream cone
☐ Key
☐ Kite
☐ Lawn mower
☐ Pirate
☐ Pizza slice
☐ Ring

☐ Sailboat
☐ Sock
☐ Tennis racket
☐ Tent
☐ Tire
☐ TV set
☐ Umbrella
☐ Yo-yo